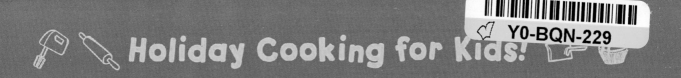

CHRISTMAS
Sweets and Treats

By Ruth Owen

WINDMILL
BOOKS

New York

Y0-BQN-229

Published in 2013 by Windmill Books, An Imprint of Rosen Publishing
29 East 21st Street, New York, NY 10010

Copyright © 2013 by Windmill Books, An Imprint of Rosen Publishing

All rights reserved. No part of this book may be reproduced in any form without permission in writting from the publisher, except by a reviewer.

First Edition

Produced for Windmill by Ruby Tuesday Books Ltd
Editor for Ruby Tuesday Books Ltd: Mark J. Sachner
US Editor: Sara Antill
Designer: Emma Randall

Photo Credits:
Cover, 1, 3, 4–5, 6–7, 8–9, 10–11, 12–13, 14–15, 16–17, 18–19, 20–21, 22–23, 24–25, 26–27, 28–29, 30–31 © Shutterstock.

Library of Congress Cataloging-in-Publication Data

Owen, Ruth, 1967–
 Christmas sweets and treats / by Ruth Owen.
     p. cm. — (Holiday cooking for kids!)
 Includes index.
 ISBN 978-1-4488-8081-2 (library binding) — ISBN 978-1-4488-8128-4 (pbk.) — ISBN 978-1-4488-8134-5 (6-pack)
 1. Christmas cooking—Juvenile literature. 2. Desserts—Juvenile literature. I. Title.
 TX739.2.C45O98 2013
 641.5'686—dc23

                              2012009780

Manufactured in the United States of America

CPSIA Compliance Information: Batch # B3S12WM: For Further Information contact Windmill Books, New York, New York at 1-866-478-0556

Contents

A Festive Time All Over the World

For billions of people worldwide, even those who do not celebrate Jesus' birth, Christmas is a beloved part of their **culture**.

Throughout most of the world, Christmas Day falls on December 25. For Christians in some countries, however, the holiday falls on January 7. The identity of Santa Claus is also different throughout the world, where he may be known as Kris Kringle, St. Nicholas, Saint Nick, Father Christmas, and other names. Even Santa's clothing hasn't always been what it is today. Did you know that his fur-lined suit was once green, not red?

Today, many **traditions** have been added to Christmas. These include brightly decorated trees and buildings, gift giving, and special food.

The recipes in this book will give you some great treats to prepare and share at Christmas. You might even want to use some of them as festive gifts!

Before you start cooking, check out all the tips and information on the following pages.

Before You Begin Cooking

Get Ready to Cook
- Wash your hands using soap and hot water. This will help to keep bacteria away from your food.
- Make sure the kitchen countertop and all your equipment is clean.
- Read the recipe carefully before you start cooking. If you don't understand a step, ask an adult to help you.
- Gather all the ingredients and equipment you will need.

Safety First!
It's very, very important to have an adult around whenever you do any of the following tasks in the kitchen:

1. Operating machinery or turning on kitchen appliances such as a mixer, food processor, blender, stovetop burners, or the oven.

2. Using sharp utensils, such as knives, can openers, or vegetable peelers.

3. Working with hot pots, pans, or cookie sheets.

Colander

Mixing bowl

Saucepan

Rolling pin

Knife

Frying pan

Cutting board

Wooden spoon

You will need these kitchen utensils to make the recipes in this book.

Sieve

Electric hand mixer

Oven mitt

Cupcake pan

Cookie sheet

Whisk

Spatula

Measuring Counts!

Measure your ingredients carefully. If you get a measurement wrong, it could affect how successful your dish turns out to be. Measuring cups and spoons are two of the most important pieces of equipment in a kitchen.

Measuring cup

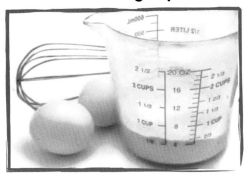

Measuring Cups

Measuring cups are used to measure the volume, or amount, of liquid or dry ingredients. Measuring cups usually hold from 1 cup to 4 cups. If you have a 1-cup measuring cup, that should be fine for all the recipes in this book. Measuring cups have markings on them that show how many cups or parts of a cup you are measuring.

Measuring Spoons

Like measuring cups, measuring spoons are used to measure the volume of liquid or dry ingredients, only in smaller amounts. Measuring spoons come in sets with different spoons for teaspoons, tablespoons, and smaller parts.

Measuring spoons

Cooking Techniques

Here are some tasks that anyone who is following directions for cooking should be sure to understand.

Bringing to a boil

Heating a liquid or mixture in a saucepan on the stovetop until it is bubbling.

Simmering

First bringing a liquid or mixture to a boil, and then turning down the heat so it's just at or below the boiling point and the bubbling has nearly stopped.

Preheating

Heating the oven until it has reached the temperature required for the recipe.

All of these tasks require the use of heat, so you should be absolutely sure to have an adult around when you do them.

Gingerbread Christmas Trees

The custom of decorating trees goes back for centuries. In some ancient cultures, people may have believed that when trees lost their leaves in winter, it meant the spirits living in the trees had also left. To lure the spirits back, people would decorate the trees with colorful pieces of cloth. When the leaves grew back in spring, people believed the tree spirits had returned because the trees looked beautiful.

Over the centuries, Christians took over the custom of hanging bright decorations at Christmastime. In the 1500s, Germans brought Christmas trees indoors, hanging apples, sweets, gingerbread, and beads on their trees. Here is a recipe that combines two holiday traditions—Christmas trees and gingerbread cookies!

You will need – ingredients:

½ cup (1 stick) butter, softened

½ cup packed brown sugar

2 large eggs

¾ cup molasses

4½ cups all-purpose flour

1 tablespoon ground cinnamon

2 teaspoons ground ginger

¼ teaspoon ground cloves

1¼ teaspoons baking powder

White, red, green, and assorted other colors of ready-to-use decorating icing tubes

M&M's or other round colored candies, sprinkles for decorating

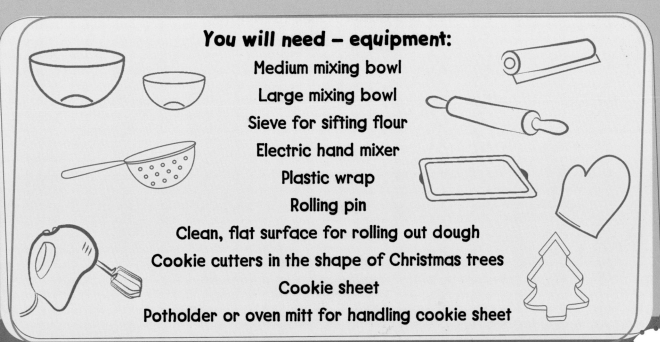

You will need – equipment:

Medium mixing bowl

Large mixing bowl

Sieve for sifting flour

Electric hand mixer

Plastic wrap

Rolling pin

Clean, flat surface for rolling out dough

Cookie cutters in the shape of Christmas trees

Cookie sheet

Potholder or oven mitt for handling cookie sheet

Step-by-Step:

Remember to ask an adult for help when you are using the electric hand mixer and oven.

1. In the large mixing bowl, use the electric mixer to blend together the butter and brown sugar. Add the eggs, one at a time, and then the molasses. Beat the mixture as you add each ingredient.

2. In the medium bowl, sift together the flour, cinnamon, ginger, cloves, and baking powder.

3. Gradually add the flour mixture to the molasses mixture, beating with the mixer until it's just blended. The dough should be stiff.

4. Divide the dough in half. Shape each half into a ball, wrap in plastic wrap, and cool in the refrigerator for one hour or in the freezer for 30 minutes, or until the dough is firm enough to roll flat. If the dough becomes too stiff, let it soften for 10 minutes at room temperature.

5. Ask an adult to help you preheat the oven to 350°F (175°C).

6. Place each ball of chilled dough on a flat, lightly floured surface and roll out until they are about ¼ inch (6 mm) thick.

7. Cut the Christmas tree shapes out of the dough with your cookie cutter.

Happy Holidays Eating

There are several stories about how Christmas trees became an American tradition. Most stories trace the custom to Germans who came to Canada and the United States in the 1700s and 1800s. The tradition took root and today nearly 40 million Christmas trees are bought each year in the United States alone!

Step-by-Step:

8. Place the cookies 1 inch (2.5 cm) apart on the cookie sheet and bake in the preheated oven for 10 minutes, or until lightly browned. Take out to cool.

9. When the cookies are cool, they're ready to decorate! Use the decorating icing and candies to give the cookies different colors, designs, and decorations.

10. You should have plenty of cookies to eat, offer guests, or take along to a holiday party!

Candy Cane Cookies

Did you ever wonder why candy canes are shaped the way they are? Some say they **symbolize** the **staffs** of the shepherds tending their sheep the night of Jesus' birth. Others say each cane is an upside-down "J," the first letter of Jesus' name.

Whatever you wish to believe, you can use this recipe to make peppermint-flavored candy cane cookies that are delicious to eat and pretty to look at hanging on your tree!

Happy Holidays Eating

One explanation for the shape of candy canes that is hard to argue with is that they are perfectly designed to hang on the branches of Christmas trees. This is thought to have happened in Europe, in the 1600s, when people first started using decorated trees as part of their Christmas celebration.

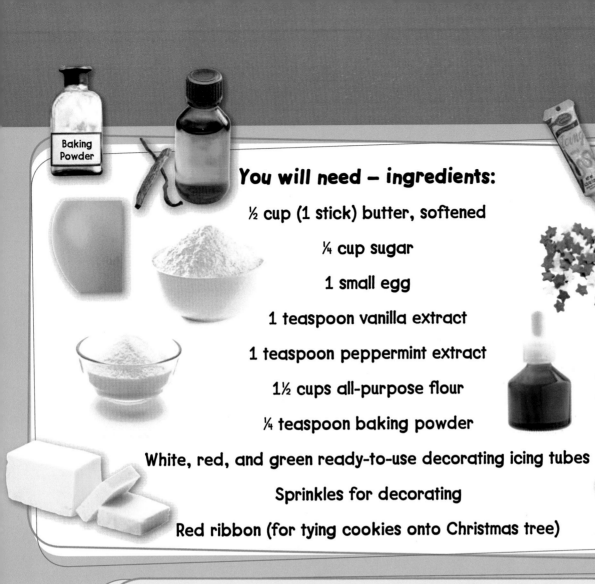

You will need – ingredients:

½ cup (1 stick) butter, softened

¼ cup sugar

1 small egg

1 teaspoon vanilla extract

1 teaspoon peppermint extract

1½ cups all-purpose flour

¼ teaspoon baking powder

White, red, and green ready-to-use decorating icing tubes

Sprinkles for decorating

Red ribbon (for tying cookies onto Christmas tree)

You will need – equipment:

Large mixing bowl

Electric hand mixer

Plastic wrap

Rolling pin

Clean, flat surface for rolling out dough

Cookie cutter in the shape of candy cane

Cookie sheet

Potholder or oven mitt for handling cookie sheet

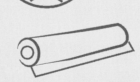

Remember to ask an adult for help when you are using the electric hand mixer and oven.

Step-by-Step:

1. Using the electric mixer, beat the butter and sugar together until creamy in the mixing bowl, and then add the egg, vanilla extract, and peppermint extract and beat until well blended.

2. Gradually add the flour and baking powder, and beat until it's just blended.

3. Shape the dough into a ball, wrap in plastic wrap, and cool in the refrigerator for an hour or in the freezer for 30 minutes.

4. Ask an adult to help you preheat the oven to 350°F (175°C).

5. Place the chilled dough on a flat, lightly floured surface and roll out until it's about ¼ inch (6 mm) thick.

6. Cut the candy cane shapes out of the dough with your cookie cutter.

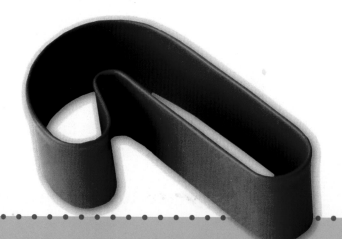

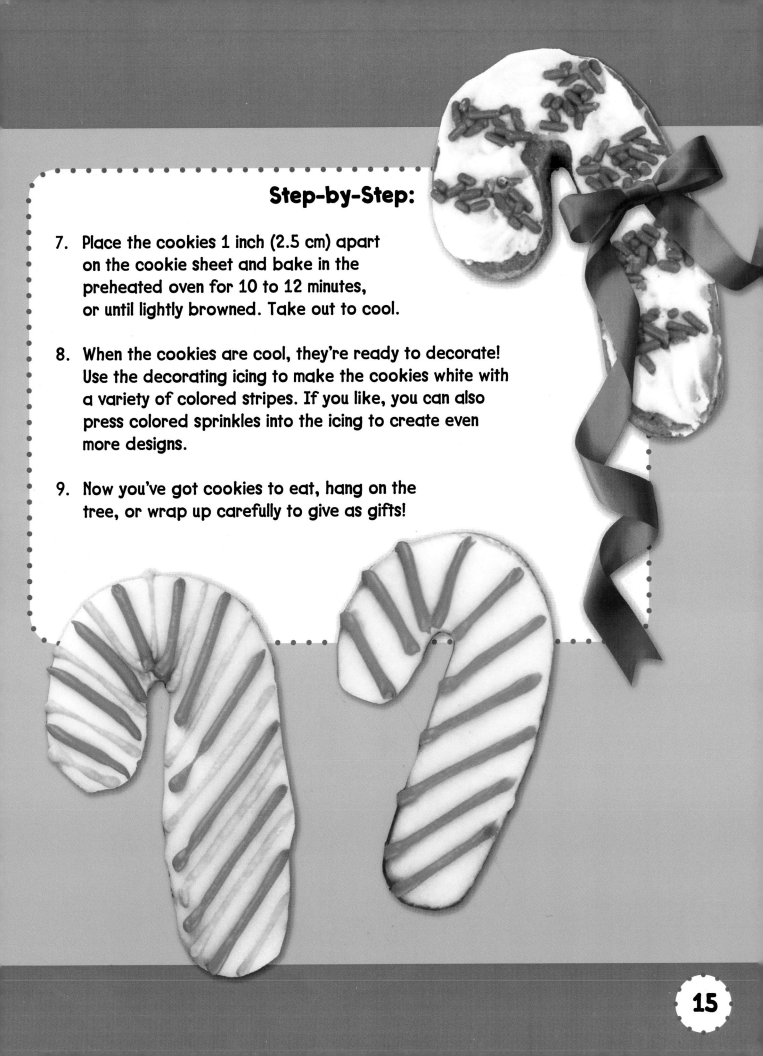

Step-by-Step:

7. Place the cookies 1 inch (2.5 cm) apart on the cookie sheet and bake in the preheated oven for 10 to 12 minutes, or until lightly browned. Take out to cool.

8. When the cookies are cool, they're ready to decorate! Use the decorating icing to make the cookies white with a variety of colored stripes. If you like, you can also press colored sprinkles into the icing to create even more designs.

9. Now you've got cookies to eat, hang on the tree, or wrap up carefully to give as gifts!

Santa's Reindeer Cupcakes

According to tradition, on Christmas Eve Santa sets off from the North Pole to deliver gifts all over the world. His sleigh is pulled by a team of flying reindeer named Dasher, Dancer, Prancer, Vixen, Comet, Cupid, Donner (or Donder), and Blitzen. The names of Santa's eight reindeer first appeared in the 1823 poem "A Visit from St. Nicholas," which is also known as "Twas the Night Before Christmas."

In 1929, a children's story by Robert L. May introduced the world to Rudolph, the reindeer who saves the day by using his shiny red nose to guide the sleigh on a foggy Christmas Eve. Now, you can bake your own reindeer team, and don't forget the red M&M's for Rudolph's nose!

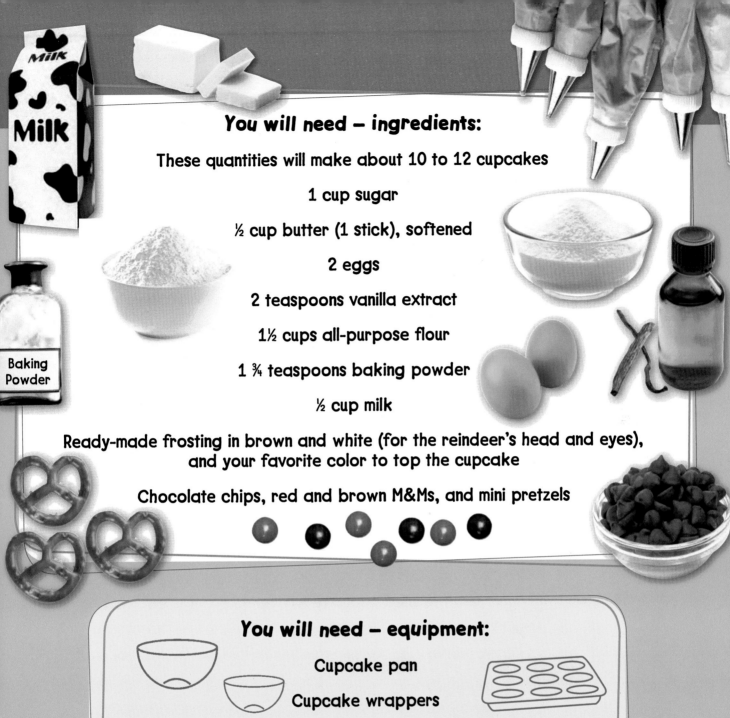

You will need – ingredients:

These quantities will make about 10 to 12 cupcakes

1 cup sugar

½ cup butter (1 stick), softened

2 eggs

2 teaspoons vanilla extract

1½ cups all-purpose flour

1 ¾ teaspoons baking powder

½ cup milk

Ready-made frosting in brown and white (for the reindeer's head and eyes), and your favorite color to top the cupcake

Chocolate chips, red and brown M&Ms, and mini pretzels

You will need – equipment:

Cupcake pan

Cupcake wrappers

Large mixing bowl

Wooden spoon for stirring

Sieve for sifting flour

Medium mixing bowl

Electric hand mixer

Toothpick

Potholder or oven mitt for handling cupcake pan

Remember to ask an adult for help when you are using the electric hand mixer and oven.

Step-by-Step:

1. Preheat the oven to 350°F (175°C).

2. Line the cupcake pan with the cupcake wrappers.

3. In the large mixing bowl, use the electric mixer to mix together the sugar and butter.

4. One at a time, beat the eggs into the sugar and butter mixture, then stir in the vanilla extract.

5. In the medium bowl, sift together the flour and baking powder.

6. Add the flour mixture to the creamy mixture and mix thoroughly.

7. Add the milk, stirring until the batter is smooth.

8. Pour the batter into the lined cupcake wrappers so that each cup is about 2/3 full.

Happy Holidays Eating

Caribou, or reindeer, live in huge herds in parts of Greenland and in northern Russia, North America, and Europe. Native people in these regions, such as the Sami of Finland, have herded caribou and eaten their meat for centuries. The caribou roam wild and the herders live a **nomadic** life moving from place to place with the animals.

Step-by-Step:

9. Bake for 20–25 minutes, until the cupcakes are light brown. Test to see if they're done by sticking a toothpick into the center of a cupcake. If it comes out clean, your cupcakes are ready. Allow the cupcakes to cool.

10. Now it's time to create your reindeers! Cover the top of each cupcake with frosting in the color of your choice.

11. Make the reindeer's head from one or two blobs of brown frosting.

12. Make the reindeer's eyes from small dots of frosting or chocolate chips.

13. Add a red or brown M&M for a nose and use mini pretzels for antlers.

Swedish Meatballs

Everyone loves a good **smorgasbord,** where people serve themselves from a large assortment of dishes. In Sweden, smorgasbords are a Christmas Eve tradition. One favorite smorgasbord offering is meatballs, called *köttbullar* in Swedish. Swedish meatballs may be served with boiled potatoes, small pickles, and lingonberry jam, which is made from a fruit grown in the forests of Sweden. Make these Swedish meatballs as a special Christmas dinner for your family. They taste great with their own sauce over potatoes, noodles, or rice!

You will need – ingredients:

1 cup fine bread crumbs

1/3 cup milk

¼ cup minced or finely chopped onion

1 pound (0.5 kg) ground beef

1 egg, beaten

1½ teaspoon salt

1/8 teaspoon pepper

½ teaspoon ground nutmeg

2 tablespoons butter

2 teaspoons flour

1 cup canned beef stock

1 cup half-and-half

You will need – equipment:

Knife

Mixing bowl

2 wooden spoons (for mixing raw ingredients and stirring cooked ingredients)

Medium covered saucepan or frying pan

Spatula or slotted spoon

Plate

Potholder or oven mitt for handling saucepan

Remember to ask an adult for help when you are handling raw meat and using the knife and the stovetop.

Step-by-Step:

1. In the mixing bowl, soak breadcrumbs in the milk.

2. Add onion, ground beef, egg, salt, pepper, and nutmeg, and mix ingredients thoroughly with wooden spoon.

3. Making sure your hands are washed, shape the meat mixture into 1 inch (2.5 cm) balls.

Uncooked meatballs

4. Melt butter in pan over low to medium heat and add meatballs.

5. Using the other wooden spoon to move the meatballs around the pan, fry until they are lightly browned on all sides.

6. Using a spatula or slotted spoon, remove meatballs from pan and set aside on clean plate.

cooked meatballs

7. Add flour to the juices from the meat and butter in pan and blend with spoon to make sauce. (Add a little more butter if mixture seems too dry.)

8. Add beef stock and half-and-half.

9. Cook and stir over medium heat for about two minutes or until sauce is smooth and lightly thickened.

Step-by-Step:

10. Add meatballs, cover, and simmer for about 15 minutes, until meatballs are cooked thoroughly. (You might want to cut into one of the meatballs before removing from pan to be sure it's not pink on the inside.)

11. You can serve your meatballs with rice or wide noodles, or eat them the traditional Swedish way with potatoes. Cranberry sauce is a good substitute for lingonberry jam.

Safety Tips for Cooking with Raw Meat

Preventing the spread of germs from raw meat is easy if you follow these simple steps:

- Use separate utensils, such as knives, spoons, dishes, and containers, for cooked and raw meat.

- Wash your hands every time you touch raw meat.

- Never put cooked food on a plate or surface that's had raw meat on it.

- Keep raw meat in a sealed container away from foods that are ready to eat, such as salads and bread.

- Fully thaw any frozen meat before you cook it.

Chocolate Truffles for Giving

In the late 1800s, expert chocolate chefs, or **chocolatiers,** in France and Switzerland combined solid milk chocolate and cream and invented a delicious new concoction that they called ganache. They then encased the velvety ganache in chocolate or cocoa powder to create a new candy. This luxurious new delicacy became known as a truffle.

This Christmas, wow your friends and family with your chocolatier skills and make homemade chocolate truffles to give as Christmas gifts.

You will need – ingredients:

To make the truffles:

1½ cups semi-sweet chocolate chips

¾ cup heavy cream

To coat the truffles:

¼ cup unsweetened cocoa powder

¼ cup granulated sugar

¼ cup chopped nuts (your choice—green pistachio nuts look festive)

¼ cup finely shredded coconut

Sprinkles

You will need – equipment:

Small saucepan

Hand whisk

Medium bowl

Small bowls (one for each different coating)

Tablespoon

Truffle wrappers

Wrapping paper or colored tissue paper, waxed paper, and ribbon (for gift-wrapping)

Step-by-Step:

Remember to ask an adult for help when you are using the stove.

1. To make the ganache for your chocolate truffles, put the chocolate chips and cream into the saucepan and simmer on the stove at a medium heat.

2. When you see tiny bubbles appear at the edges of the cream, turn off the heat.

3. Let the mixture sit for 3 to 4 minutes while the chocolate melts in the hot cream.

4. Combine the chocolate and cream using the hand whisk. Keep gently whisking until the mixture is smooth and shiny.

5. Pour the ganache into a bowl and put into the refrigerator until the mixture becomes solid. This will take at least 2 hours.

Happy Holidays Eating

The chocolate truffle got its name because its makers thought it looked like a type of small wild mushroom that grows under trees in some forests. In France, these wild mushrooms are named "truffles," so the new candies took this name, too.

Step-by-Step:

6. Mix the cocoa powder and granulated sugar and put into a small bowl. Put the nuts, sprinkles, and coconut into individual bowls.

7. Using a tablespoon, take a spoonful of ganache. Roll the ganache into a ball using your fingers. Be sure to wash your hands first!

8. Roll the ball of ganache in one of the toppings until it is completely coated. Put the truffle into a truffle wrapper.

9. To gift-wrap the truffles, place a square of wrapping paper or colored tissue paper on a flat surface. Put a square of waxed paper on top (to protect the gift-wrapping). Arrange some truffles in the center of the waxed paper. Pull up the paper around the truffles, scrunch the ends together to make a bag, and tie with a ribbon (see picture on page 24).

10. Refrigerate the truffles until you are ready to give them or eat them.

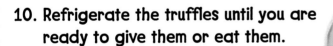

Eggless Eggnog

With origins in Britain, eggnog has long been a favorite holiday drink throughout North America. Eggnog was traditionally made with raw eggs. Today it's made in ways that are safer than eating raw eggs and suitable for people who have an **allergy** to eggs. Here's an eggless recipe that will give you and your friends a rich, thick, and creamy glass of Christmas cheer!

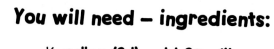

You will need – ingredients:

½ gallon (2 l) cold 2% milk

3.4-ounce (96-g) package instant French vanilla pudding mix

¼ cup sugar

3 teaspoons vanilla extract

1 teaspoon ground cinnamon

1 teaspoon ground nutmeg

Cinnamon sticks and whipped cream
(for decorating if required)

You will need – equipment:

Large mixing bowl

Wooden spoon

Large airtight container

Pitcher or large bowl with ladle for serving

Cups or drinking glasses
for drinking

Step-by-Step:

1. In the mixing bowl, mix together 2 cups cold milk and pudding mix and stir until smooth.

2. Add sugar, vanilla extract, cinnamon, and nutmeg, and stir until all the ingredients are blended. Make sure to scrape the side of the bowl while stirring so everything is blended smoothly.

3. Stir in remaining milk slowly.

4. Pour into airtight container and refrigerate for 30 minutes to thicken. Stir well before serving in a pitcher or bowl with a ladel.

5. If you like, you may add some whipped cream, sprinkle a little extra cinnamon or nutmeg on top of each serving, and decorate with a cinnamon stick.

TIP:
For a thicker drink, increase pudding mix to 2 boxes. For fewer calories, use sugar-free pudding.

Wassail (Apple Cider Punch)

The word *wassail* (pronounced WAH-suhl) comes from ancient England, where wassailing ceremonies were held to encourage a good harvest in the late fall. The beverage that people drank during those celebrations was also called wassail. Wassailing can also mean going house to house singing Christmas carols, and today the drink is a wonderful way to welcome friends who stop by during the holiday season!

You will need – ingredients:

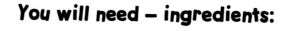

½ gallon (2 l) apple cider

2 cups fresh orange juice (with some pulp)

½ cup freshly squeezed lemon juice

12 whole cloves

4 cinnamon sticks

1 pinch (just under 1/8 teaspoon) ground ginger

1 pinch (just under 1/8 teaspoon) ground nutmeg

1 orange, thinly sliced

You will need – equipment:

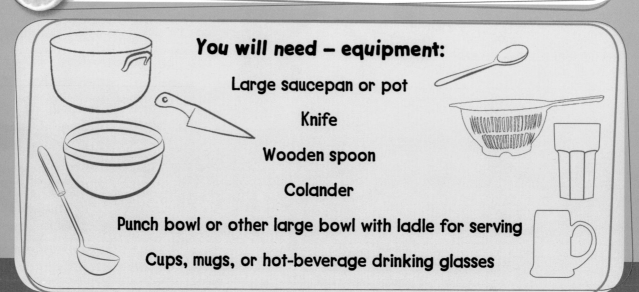

Large saucepan or pot

Knife

Wooden spoon

Colander

Punch bowl or other large bowl with ladle for serving

Cups, mugs, or hot-beverage drinking glasses

Step-by-Step:

Remember to ask an adult for help when you are working with the knife, the hot stovetop, and the hot drinks.

1. In the large pot over low heat, combine apple cider, orange juice, and lemon juice.

2. Add cloves, cinnamon sticks, ginger, nutmeg, and orange slices, and stir to blend all the ingredients. Set aside a few cinnamon sticks and orange slices to serve with drinks, if desired.

3. Bring to a simmer and allow to simmer for about 45 minutes, stirring occasionally.

4. Before serving, if desired, use ladle or measuring cup to pour mixture through the colander into the bowl to strain out the solid ingredients. Or all of the mixture may be poured into the punch bowl, and guests may serve themselves with the ladle.

5. Serve hot from punch bowl.

6. If you like, you may add a cinnamon stick and orange slice to each cup.

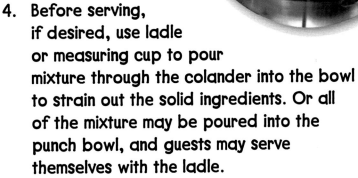

Glossary

21982320285020

allergy (A-lur-jee) When a person's body reacts badly to something such as a type of food or an animal. An allergy may make a person vomit, get sore skin, sneeze, or become seriously ill.

chocolatier (CHAH-kuh-leh-TEER) A person who makes candies and chocolate figures such as Easter eggs, from chocolate.

culture (KUL-chur) All the ways in which a group of people live and express themselves, such as dress, food, art, language, music, and celebrations.

nomadic (noh-MA-dik) Moving around; not staying in one place, usually in order to find new places to live or to raise livestock.

smorgasbord (SMOR-gus-bohrd) A buffet, or meal consisting of several dishes from which people may serve themselves.

staff (STAF) A long stick used as a support while walking or climbing, as a weapon, or as a shepherd's crook, to help control sheep and other animals.

symbolize (SIM-buh-lyz) To stand for or represent something else, such as an important event or person. A cross may be a symbol of Christianity.

tradition (truh-DIH-shun) A practice that a group of people have performed for many years and that passes on to the people who come after them.

Index

Websites

For web resources related to the subject of this book, go to: www.windmillbooks.com/weblinks and select this book's title.